AF439460

I'M JUST HERE FOR DISPLAY

A COLLECTION OF POEMS

Kirsten Pratt and
Clarke Peters

ISBN: 9798838739483

DEDICATIONS

To my husband who has supported me throughout my writing process; Reading every single word, providing endless encouragement, being my biggest cheerleader, and my number one fan. You see worth and purpose in anything I have to say, even when I struggle to. I love you always.

- Kirsten

To my husband. Some of these are about you.

- Clarke

CONTENTS

CONTENTS

CONTENTS

INTRODUCTION

Life is so peculiar. People come into your life and trample all over your heart, then leave. But some people come at the most unexpected times and they get to stay forever. Life is exciting and devastating and unpredictable. You'll make plans and have dreams that never come to fruition. Sometimes what will come in their place is heartache and ruin. But sometimes, miraculous things happen. Things that were so far out of reach, you couldn't even begin to dream of them.

Here you'll find nostalgia and darkness; A scared inner child and the assertive woman she grew into. You'll find love, sex, death and despair; Hopes and dreams and fairytales. My wish is that something here - a word, a phrase, an entire poem - will resonate with you. That you'll feel seen, heard, and understood. As life is a collective experience, I hope these stories can be too. So whether we all used to make potions out of rocks and leaves, or dreamt of having a baby, or were dramatic pre-teens; My hope is that something draws you to it, and keep it with you.

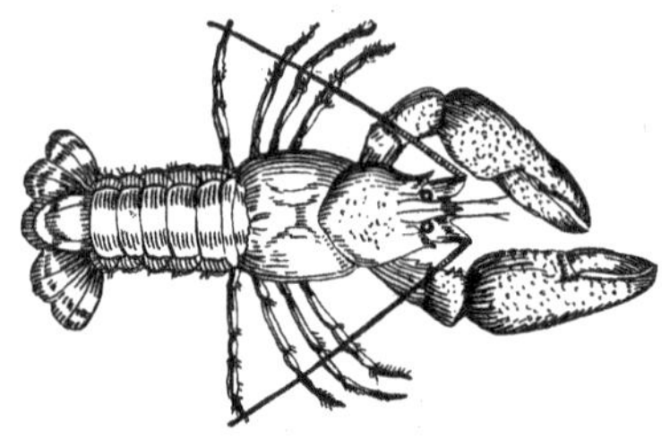

I used to walk along the river,
Chasing the water as it flowed between smooth
stones,
Watching the small minnows dart out of my way.
I'd dig deep under big rocks and flip them.
I'd find silly crawdads and watch them.
They'd scurry backwards as I scooped them up,
And avoided their sharp pinchers.
I'd mimic them.
Throw my torso under water,
And propel myself backwards.
Kicking up small pebbles,
Creating small waves under the already flowing
water,
Laughing, like I'd never had so much fun in my
entire life.

I would search and search
For the flattest, smoothest stone I could find.
Many were considered,
But they ker-plunked as they were tossed back.
I'd jump with joy when I found one,
Then slice it through the water.
I'd watch it leap and count each one,
As though my joy transferred to it when we touched.

I used to comb through the bordering trees,
Beasts so tall they blocked out the sun.
One would always catch my eye,
And I'd go to it,
As though it was calling me.

I'd climb as high as it's sturdy branches would allow,
Feeling my bare feet scrape against its rough skin,
And summer leaves tickle my soaked arms.
When I reached the top, a beam of light would hit me.
I would stare in wonder at the vastness.
From there, I could see just how small I was.
I'd lounge and daydream,
Allowing the birds to fill my head with music
As the sun licked clean each drop of the river left on my body.

I would gather leaves and blossoms,
Dried bark and sticks,
As I climbed back down to make a potion.
A hollowed tree stump was my cauldron.
I'd find pebbles and chestnuts, acorns and flowers.
I'd toss in each ingredient,
Stirring in water with a spoon-shaped stick.
I'd grab a handful of dirt
And throw it down as I said the magic words.
And in that instant, the potion would gain its magic.
I'd pretend to drink it down,
Hoping it would work this time.
I'd gather my courage and run back to the trailer,
Sneaking in to hide in the closet
And avoid the wrath of the monsters who lived there with me.

I was born
On a Thursday
In the middle of winter
Who knows the time
No one
Really cares anyway
The winter bit me
Like the Shepherd
Who doesn't release
When it's told
And it was then
That the icy
Bitterness
Found its way
To my small heart
At least
That's what I'm told
I'm never happy
I'm never satisfied
I'm never content
I'm just filled with contempt
I mean
If you say so
My greenish eyes
Are not like
Springtime leaves
Or summertime grass
Or even your favorite weed
They've always been dull
Mirroring
The emptiness inside
Like sorority-girl vomit
Or what you'd call envy
Interpreting jealousy
As green-light-go
I'm not allowed
To say "no"

Irish
In my blood
But I never
Came with luck
Or a pot of gold
Just deep freckles
And pinkish skin
Controlled
By the whims
Of madmen
I was born
When no one asked
If that's what I wanted
And
So I'm told
I'm made to be
How they wanted
And that's okay
Because it has to be
That's just
The way it is
No one
Really cares anyway

"Mommy, my tummy hurts."
It's a simple sentence actually,
But what I really meant was my vagina.
Well, monkey...
At least that's what I was taught to call it.
Like it's some fucking zoo animal.

You steal it from it's home
And profit off strangers coming to gawk at it.
Something you pass around for tourists to paw at,
And take pictures with to look back on in pleasure.
Something you train to do tricks for you,
Then beat it when it doesn't sit still
And do as it's told.
Something so exotic, it's illegal to own,
But that makes the bad men want it more,
And believe me,
They'll get it.

They'll get it in the dark of night
When everyone else is sleeping.
They'll get it when it's bath time
And it's their job to do the bathing.
They'll get it when you're working late
When you're out with friends, or taking a break.
They'll get it in the middle of the day
When they've gotten brave
And everyone else is in the kitchen
Making that little girls' birthday cake.

And she'll smile
She'll do as she's told.
She's a good and quiet little girl.
She won't let her fear show,
When he comes for her in the night.
She'll cover what she can
With bubbles during bath time,
And do her best to ignore what's happening
On the other side of the shower curtain.
She'll pray you don't have to work late today
Or need a break from her with your friends.
But when you do, she'll lie still on the bed
Suffocating on the sweat and seeing red.
And her last shred of hope will wither away
On her fucking birthday, when he got brave.
Because she knew then, that you knew,
It wasn't really her tummy that hurt.

Small and alone
In a new world
A sea of strange faces
A carrot-haired girl

She has speckled freckles
And a kind smile
She calls me over
Asks me to stay a while

Nervous but brave
I follow her lead
"We're best friends"
She assertively decreed

On that day
In second grade
I met the person
Who would help me find my purpose

And though we grew up
And life sent us separate ways
I still think of her fondly
And miss the good old days

Innocent, that was me
Before I met you.
Naive, longing
For someone to love me.
Then you came along
And showed me the way.

How could you take me
And change me into someone I'm not?
Why did you choose me
Then take me in, just to tear me up?
Who do you think you are
To steal me and my innocence away?

So confused, not myself
Now that I have you.
So in love, I was oblivious
Of what you came to do.
Who is this beast
That captured my essence
And left me void
Of everything I once knew?

How could you take me
And change me into someone I'm not?
Why did you choose me
Then take me in, just to tear me up?
Who do you think you are
To steal me and my innocence away?
How could I fall for the games
That everyone said you would play?

Lonely, broken
Now that you're gone.
Who is this ghost, staring back at me?
How can I get myself back?

10

The sky is falling all around me
My hands are shaking
And I can't breathe
Your eyes are on me
My head is spinning
My knees are trembling at your touch
Oh, I think I've got a crush

130 pounds
That's how big I am
Big enough
To fight my demons
Strong enough
To shove them under my bed
Old enough
To tell them how much I'm worth
Audacious enough
To tell them where to shove it

You were a windy road up a mountain with steep
cliffsides
Your jagged turns were sharp and cut like knives
Sharper still were the eggshells you'd leave in your
wake
The smallest mistakes were deadly
And you always seemed to find fault
I used to want to be just like you, spontaneous and
free
Until I grew up, saw the anger and depression you'd
soon pass down to me

I was far too young to see the cycle
I clung to your mania, while bracing for the spiral
Your inexplicable happiness would flip to madness
on a dime
I'd internalize your hatred for yourself like it was a
victimless crime
I would pray you would sleep as you dipped down
low
And I wouldn't dare wake the beast, so I'd creep
really slow
And I still had hope that this time you'd wake and be
different
But no matter what, I was insignificant

I wanted you to love me
But you loved your illness more
I begged for you to get better
But you thought the pills made you a bore
I tried to throw you a lifeboat
But you just made me the scapegoat
So over time, I grew up and stopped trying
I chose myself, and you're still justifying
But it's different now, because no one's listening
The weight of you is no longer crippling

Will I sit alone and suffer in silence
For yet another night?
Will I be brave enough to relinquish
The sliver of control
I have over this chaos?
I am consumed by the anxiety
And shame
And guilt
But the reflection in the mirror
Scolds me into refusing to be a burden

And I pinch
And I twist
And I bind
And I suck in
And I don't breathe
So I can wear jeans
Causing pretty red lines
And I chop my thighs
To match the gap in my teeth
That I force to close
Then slather in bleach
And I fill my lips
And I lift my breasts
And I tuck my chin
Because bruised is better
Than curves in the wrong places
And I extend my lashes
And I slice my brows
And I tan my skin
Until I look like the collage of girls
In your magazines
But even still
The mirror shows
Some other imperfection
I can fix
With enough money
And some plastic

15

Warm grass
Goosebumps
Summer heat
A little treat

Strawberries and chocolate
Melting on my skin
You want a taste
Should I make you wait?

Honeysuckle
Honey bees
Honey lips
Summer breeze

Watermelon seeds
Sweet iced tea
Dazzling smiles
Won't you stay for a while?

Tire swing
Big oak tree
Wind in my hair
Anticipation in the air

Sunflower maze
You love to chase, but
I have to be earned
Haven't you learned?

Splashing water
Cannonballs
Glistening skin
Makes his head spin

Dancing and playing
In tall grass fields
You think to yourself
"Oh the power she wields"

Every year
A new town, new name
A new toy to play with
Every single day

Summer love
Three months of fun
Carefree, spontaneous
And sex, a ton!

But forever?
It's just not for me
You see, I prefer
To just be free

Hold my hand
My fingers are lonely
Without yours there
Hold me tight
My body is cold
Without you by my side
Love me strong
We both know
You won't be here in the morning

You'll leave me here
Like you always do
While I'm fast asleep
Dreaming of you
You'll kiss me goodbye
And I won't wake up
Because you do this all the time
I'm not your only one

Sometimes I daydream
About the life we could have
If I was better,
If I was enough for you
I'd do my hair how you like
I'd wear the clothes you picked for me
I'd keep my body in shape
I'd make your favorite meals
I'd take your scraps happily
I'll believe it means you love me
Just, please

Don't leave me here
Just hold my hand
While I dream of you
Dream of me too
Don't kiss me goodbye
Instead, hold me tight
Even though we both know
I'm not the One

DETOX

We all have our fixes, some stranger than others
You loved your drugs, it gave the world more color
Ecstasy, acid, especially weed
On top of the alcohol and occasional amphetamines

You tried to hide it and rarely would you succeed
I'd always find your stash, the pipe, or the money
Feeling so stupid for giving you the benefit of the
doubt
Truly believing the money had just been lost or that
my eyes had been deceived

I hated those drugs, they were always more important
than me
You'd beg me to stay and help you get clean
So we would begin the process every few months
To get you sober, it was really tough

I'd become a punching bag when your emotions
flipped
Long nights, no sleep, and poor appetites
For once you needed me, and I loved to feel needed
We made it through so many times
And I always believed we had succeeded

Until one day when our life together wasn't enough
You needed yet another chemically induced rush
You threw away my trust each time you used
But still I was there, to help you get through
Like I said, everyone has their fix
His was drugs, and he never could stay sober
Maybe mine was feeling needed
And believing one day the addiction could be over

19

Dark bar
Dark music
Dark wine

Dark mood
Dark makeup
Dark dress

Dark hair
Dark eyes
Dark grin

Dark humor
Dark dance
Dark kiss

Dark room
Dark sheets
Dark moans

Dark fist
Dark blood
Dark groans

Dark night
Dark dumpster
Dark news

Dark box
Dark gowns
Dark cries

Dark bar
Dark grins
Dark habits

Loving you is a special kind of torture
To see your face, and not kiss it
To hug you, and have to let go
To see your heart, and not call it mine
To look in the mirror, and like myself less
Without you

The stars in your eyes
Match the galaxies in mine
It's like the planets aligned
Igniting my body afire
And the pull of gravity is just...

Relentless
Luxurious
Suffocating
Exhilarating

A black hole
The singularity of you
Enveloping me all at once
And tearing me to shreds

Celestial and Radiant
You shower down on me
In fireballs of meteors
I relish in the beauty
And ignore the flames
Licking at my skin

You always knew how to leave a mark

22

My hips on your lips
And your fingertips
On my taunt nips

My hands in your hair
And we don't have a care
In the world

You love it when
I ride your face
And drip, drip, drip
Like ocean waves

And as my waves begin to swell
You come bursting all over me

I cried this morning
Because he wasn't you
I closed my eyes this morning
And traced his lips
But my mind traced yours
If I could make him feel like you, I would
But, I can't
Which is why I cried this morning

A penny for your thoughts
A nickel for a smile
He's a dime a dozen
And yet, he thinks he's worthwhile
He'll exchange a quarter for a moment of pleasantries
Then think I want a dollar for my name
But when I politely decline his tips
I'll learn what he really hoped to gain

Flashing his dollar
He reminds me I'm only 82 cents
And since he's worth more than me
I should apologize for my offense
Besides
He provided me with the honor of his presence
I owe him
I'm indebted to his "kindness"
"I'm a nice guy" he says
So that means I must relent

Round and round we go
Like money being spent
Even when I stand my ground
I'm just playing hard to get
Name dropping a fancy restaurant
He thinks he can buy my time
Like slipping a dollar into the panties of a stripper
And expecting their full attention, Showtime

But what he doesn't know is
The cost of just existing as a woman
Far exceeds the means he believes he has
And when he finally understands
That what he wants is not for sale
He'll do what he does best
And justify taking it anyway
After all
He's a nice guy
And I'm just here for display

You think you're happy
You found someone you fell in love with deeply,
madly, quickly
He is like a good stiff drink, he gives the correct
perspective; not a different perspective- the corrent
one.

Maybe what I like the best about him is the way he
makes me, not makes me feel just makes me. I am his
and I love that title.

He shows me what is important in life
Before him I only wanted to assume independence,
Now for the first time I want nothing more than to
love him and be loved by him. I want every
degrading thing I use to hate.

I want to belong to him
He is strong, tender and brillant.
His hands are like a machine, so rough and regulated
but when he touches me they become gentle.

I want his hands to hold me even when theres no
logical reason why I need to be held other than to
show me that he loves me

Until tonight

The hands I crave pushed me away, shoved me and
were no longer mine while I sat loving him never any
less.

I hate a life where I lose him, where I lose who he is,
his correct perspective, his words that hurt but still
heal me
He is my poison and my wine and I will drink until
he is how I remember

My ribs are monkey bars
That are expected to hold the weight of you
As you swing carelessly until I'm raw

My lungs are a bouncy house
I inflate for you
Yet you don't have the decency
To remove your shoes before you pounce

My brain is a maze
You don't bother to get lost in
Banter used to be fun,
Like the back and forth of a see-saw
Now, my mouth is nothing
But another hole for you to fill

You expect my body to be a temple
Then disgrace it every chance you get
Until I'm an old playground
No one wants to play on anymore
And you run to find a new one to ruin

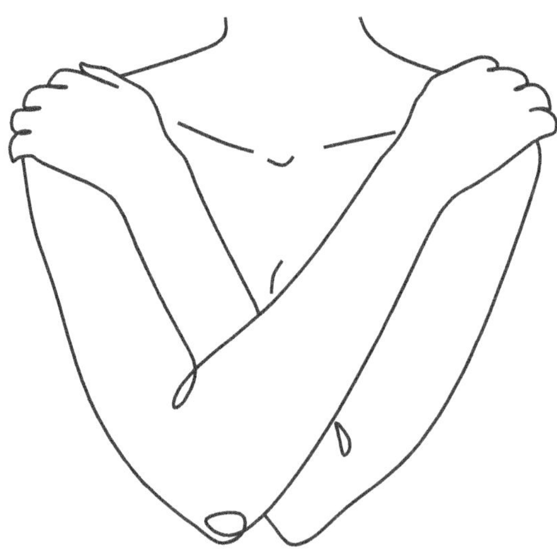

Your words are as smooth as your lips
Both of which are in my head
While I'm faced with the choice
To love or leave you

All of your promises are replaying in my head
So loudly I can barely think
But one promise screams the loudest
You promised to never leave me

Funny,
I killed myself tonight
In sacrificing everything I built for you
Because I thought you'd do the same

Funny,
At the end of the day, I cried
Not over what I gave up
But because of what I chose

I chose you
And you didn't do the same
I fell in love with your lips and your smooth words
I should've known that words are cheap
Especially when you have her lips

Give me a reason
Just one
To stay or leave
To love or grieve
To die or survive
To exist or feel alive

Give me a reason
Just one
To choose you over me
To be here or chase dreams
To save you and lose myself
To change into someone else

Give me a reason
Just one
To say "no" for once
To be okay with that
To find love for myself
To stop being a placemat

Your lack of a reason is reason enough

God took my head off
To sleep is miraculous but it rarely comes
But not without reliving the pain over again

I asked God to give me sleep and as I laid there
picturing how pathetic I looked he reached out from
the wall and took the top of my head

He took out what looked like a glowing piece of
spaghetti, twisted it around his finger and put it back
in

When he closed my head, all was black and I slept

Shattering in the borrowed light of the moon
Bowl-shaped depressions deep to my core
Cleansed by pools of salt
Lost you by sheer default

Crossed like hearts, stars, and Lovers
Fate always knew you weren't mine to keep
Broken like bones and promises, undiscovered
I knew what I was sowing, it's time to reap

Blissful ignorance means I can be happy
Pretending means nothing has to change
But I knew "Loyal" wasn't in his discription,
So why do I even feel betrayed?

You're easy to love, but hard to forget
It's easy to run, but hard to leave
Knowing that I can have you again
Makes leaving more possible
But what happens if I have to leave for good?

I never intend to find out

It started like they all do, beautiful and exciting
With the flutters, passion, and heat, so enticing
A look of lust and a stroke of luck
Had me believing that our fate on that beach had
been sealed
I had no way of knowing what time would reveal

In my mind were fantasies of
Midnight giggles
Rocking chairs
And never knowing what to have for dinner
It's always a gamble when you meet someone new
In the beginning you made me feel like a highroller
winner

My starfish wishes lead to salty kisses
Dancing in the kitchen after clearing dinners dishes
But now you look at me like I'm the detritus washed
up by the high tide
Until my reflection agrees, and all I want to do is
hide
And I feel insane because you will deny it until the
day you die
And so I lie

I lie to you and my family and friends
I continue to dream and will things to mend
I put band-aids on my cuts and duct tape over my
mouth
While I allow your hypnosis to lure me back to your
truth

And though you have me so confused, I'm happy
I can't believe my starfish wishes came true

I scrub and I scrub
But my skin still remains
A collage
Painted in shades of red shame
Blue guilt
And purple flashes of memories
Begging to be burned and forgotten

I remind myself
It wasn't all jealous nights
and stupid fights
There were times
We were so high
On happiness
Our love
A bright blinding white

I can't stop thinking about it
The familiar music fills my head on a loop
My food still taps to it
Stuck in the same trance
I can still see it
The exact moment the light ignited in your eyes
I had never seen that color soul before
And you were so easy to get lost inside of
I was blissfully unaware how trapped I was
And I remained there for so long
There was no longer a line
Where you ended and I began
The more I searched
The more hopeless it became
So I left without her
Escape was futile
I'm still ensnared
Inside an unfamiliar shell
Created in her place

And so I scrub

You cover me like skin
Maybe smother is a better word
Like an outer coat that's too hot,
Too bulky and uncomfortable
You know the kind
With no zipper
Just a hole that's much too small for my head
Too small for my body in fact
I feel suffocated
And I can't breathe
Can't move
Can't think

This feeling is fine for a second
But eventually it grows exhausting
I want you gone
So I pick

I drop a chunk of you on the ground
Finally feeling lighter
Less of you
Means more of me
I watch you pile onto the ground
Just as the air piles into my lungs
I sigh in relief
As I finally rid myself of you
Only to realize
I am bleeding

Shit
Not again

You were always so imposing
A massive shadow casting out all the light until I
burned out
Your narrowing gaze, hollow, and cold, pinning me in
place until I submitted
Your intransigent values slowly stripping me of my
own until I'm nothing
I reduce my world to words on pages
It's too big to understand any other way

I read the reflections from a girl I barely know
A girl full of life to live
A girl full of dreams to catch
A girl full of love to give
A girl giving up dreams for him
A girl dulling her life for him
A girl forced to contort and break and shrink into a
mold she'd never fit
A girl pitied into non-existence

Reading about her life, I realize
She would not have been so malleable
If it weren't for the sickeningly sweet gestures
That followed thousands of small papercuts he made
just for fun
I hope one day
She figures that out for herself
And finds the strength to get out

It's easy to make promises you think you never have
to keep
Running away isn't the same as running towards
I ran towards and you ran away
If you ran away and never returned
I'd still love you

I hate that I'd still love you
I hate that still, I love you
I hate that I love you
I love you

I love you, and you love her
And I hate that you love her
You love her, so I ran away
And I hate that I ran away

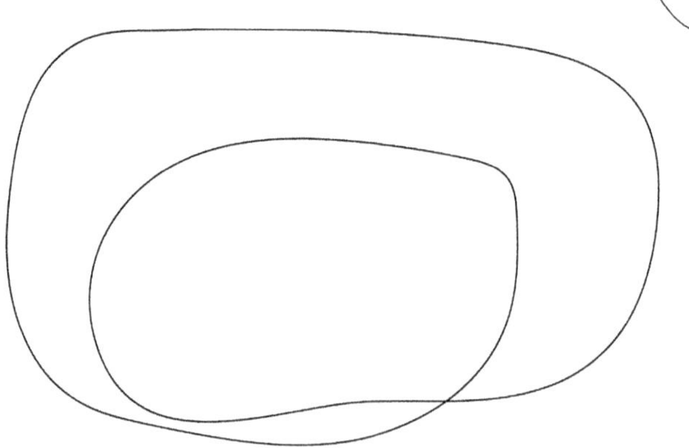

I took my Wellbutrin
Washed it down with a double shot
Of some cheap old Malibu
I probably should've already thrown out

I cleaned up my racoon eyes
With some spit and a stained rag
Pretended I knew who I was
What I was doing
Ignoring all my own red flags

I poured out all my trauma
Held against a dirty bathroom stall
By some middle-aged lonely man
I could probably call dad

I slipped the Rolex off his wrist
Shoved his wallet up my sleeve
Swallowed down the acid vomit
As he came inside of me

How much longer can you live like this?
The television preacher asks of me
As if I begged each had that's grazed me
To etch their prints into my skin
As if i created every bomb that goes off
Each time I try to mend
As if I don't look at myself with more hate
Than my mother ever will
As if I haven't tried anything different
As if I haven't tried to heal

But who could afford a therapist
With the amount of shit
I've buried deep
They'd probably lock me
In a psych ward
Drug me
Till I could finally sleep

Then they'd whisper amongst themselves
How they, too, have to give up on me
Since I am way beyond saving
And just too damaged to be seen

The wind blew through my hair
In the meadow where we fell
And the dandelions painted us like snow
With pretty pink shoulders
And angel-kissed cheeks
You mind more clear than my own
I danced on the tightrope
With no fear that I'd slip
So sure that you were my net
Then the wind blew south
The ice that slated the ground
Decided that's all of the "you" I would get

I should've kissed you ten thousand times
So I'd never forget the taste of your lips
I should've counted each fleck of gold in your eyes
Maybe then my memory would be rich
I should've soaked up the warmth in each tight hug
So I wouldn't feel so frozen right now
I should've bottled your laughter to keep for myself
Maybe then I'd feel whole again, somehow

But if I'm honest
You were too good to be true
Forced to play the hand you have
Even if they weren't the cards you drew
And though I chose you
From the very beginning, I always saw
The bold, red writing on the wall

If you're giving everything
And getting nothing in return

You're just getting screwed

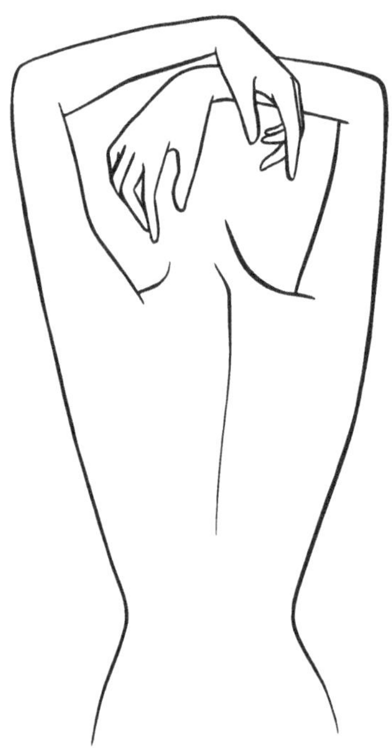

We're not talking
And you're eyes won't make contact

You're not listening
Why won't my mouth stop moving

You haven't touched me in days
But your silence slaps

Sometimes I wonder who I would be
If you hadn't come into my life.
Would I still be afraid of the dark?
Sitting frozen, petrified,
Eyes darting around the blackness,
Waiting for a figure to appear,
Heart thumping and hands fumbling for the light
switch.

Would I still spend so much time testing lighting in
hotel rooms?
Bathroom light on with the door just the right
amount cracked
Or light over the stove, or the hallway light, or the
lamp at bedside?
Trying to decide what is too bright to leave on
But too dark to sleep.
Wishing I hadn't forgotten my night light at home.
I pretend I am brave
But clearly I'm not.
Even though I'm on vacation
Hundreds of miles away
I'm still irrationally hypervigilant of you.

If it weren't for you,
Would I still cringe at the feeling of breath on my
skin?
The heat of deep sleep breathing
The brush of a sigh
The coolness of soft shushing in my ear.
My stomach turns at the thought.

I remember your subtle grooming.
A hand on my thigh and brushing hair from my neck
Turned to stripping naked and cuddling while you
took a nap,
And I'd lay there as your wiry hair pricked my skin.
I was three.
I was still a baby.
I was so small that even your breath was bigger than
me.
And I couldn't breathe.
Still, why can't I breathe?

Would spiders still give me panic attacks?
I vividly remember the tarantula in your room.
It was the only thing to look at
While the worst thing that's ever happened to me
Happened over and over again.
Maybe my fear of you was projected onto that spider
And every spider thereafter.
He never hurt me
But he watched you and did nothing to stop it
So, I guess it's his fault.

I remember when you fed him a mouse.
I couldn't bear to sit and watch,
Waiting for imminent death.
But then something amazing happened.
In a miraculous turn of events,
It was the spider who died.
Maybe of old age,
Maybe of shame.
I kept the mouse.

Maybe that's a metaphor for my life.
You were the spider,
I was the mouse.
You, the predator
Me, your prey.
But the mouse was saved
Before it could be devoured.
Unfortunately, I was not.
You didn't die of old age,
You certainly didn't die of shame
And a miracle wasn't saved for me.

It's over now,
But I'll always carry it with me.
In little bizarre fears
That on the surface, means nothing.
You'll never know what it's like
To be so self-aware
And still so consumed by irrationalities.

I guess my miracle is that I survived
Of course it's hard
But if I could survive it,
I am strong enough to talk about it.
I've learned over the years
The only person who should be uncomfortable,
Is you.
The only person who should hide,
Is you.
The only person who should be afraid,
Is you.
I can share my story with no fear,
Because the consequences belong to you.
The shame is not mine to carry.
It's yours.

Everyone wants a burning, passion-filled love
Did everyone forget that burns cause pain
Pain that causes deep wounds
Wounds that require healing
Healing that can only happen
With time and white blood cells
Both of which you just don't have enough of anymore

I'm so grateful that I stole you
Like a thief in the night
I knew I had to have you
I was sure after the first night
That I met your personality
And was introduced to your smile
Any attempt to kill the fire in my veins
Would be futile

I knew you were making promises to another
What a shame
No matter, I knew at the end
On your lips was my name

One by one, I stole each promise
And wore them like rings
And in the same way
I severed all of your frayed and fragile strings

To steal means to take something
That to me does not belong
But when you're inside of me
I know you were made for me all along
So call me what you want
But a thief I am not
For he has always belonged to me
And no one else
As you may have so incorrectly thought

Eyes like wildfire.
They alight my soul,
And burn me alive.
I relish in the heat,
In the lust.
In the beating of my heart,
As it tries to keep me alive,
While my body disintegrates.

Hands like flower petals.
They glide over my skin,
And heighten every sense.
My body anticipates their motion,
And moves in rhythm.
A slow, tantalizing dance.
The line between pleasure and pain
Blurred.

Lips like honey.
They pull back in a killer smile,
And pierce the pit in my stomach.
I long to taste them,
But they're too busy
Preparing the feast that is me
I won't complain.
They'll bring me leftovers,
When I'm finished.

And that's the best part.
I always finish

When I close my eyes, I can see it

I see white flakes falling from the heavens
Threatening to swallow the world up, whole
I hear crackling of the wood that we set on fire to
keep us warm
The yellow haze below the two stockings hanging on
our mantle
I smell apples and cinnamon burning beside us
I smell you and your soap
As I push myself deeper into the space you created
for me
I feel your arms tighten
And your thumbs drawing circles on my arm
I see you, in your red sweater that's barely visible
Under the thick blankets where we hide
I watch your eyes track the screen as you watch
Rudolph
And I watch you

When I close my eyes, I can see it

The droplets of sweat covering your brow
I see the flecks of grass stuck to your shirt
As you hurry to finish the chore before the storm
hits
I hear the mower as it placates the lawn
Turning our jungle of a house into a civilized home
I hear thunder announcing it's arrival
And I hear your footsteps announcing a much
sweeter arrival
I smell the freshly cut grass, and the threat of rain
I smell the heat coming off the pavement as the
showers start
I feel your shirt, as it clings to your back
Held on by moisture
I feel your skin, and the goosebumps forming
As the shirt releases it's hold

I feel you pull me into the water, as we allow the rain
to wash over us
I watch as you reach out, to prevent me from leaving
The storm smiling at my glee
I can see myself attempting to run indoors
Always knowing I'd run back to you if I ever got away

When I close my eyes, I can see it

I see the world washed in pinks and purples
Changed by my sunglasses
I see your skin, A trifecta of colors
White, red, and brown
I smell the salt washing over our feet
And the scent of lotion, as it fights off the rays
I hear the screams of kids playing around us
I hear you whisper "Soon"
I hear the waves hitting and the birds singing
It's as if they know a scene such as this is a cause for
music
I feel the sand between my toes
The sun massaging and warming my shoulders
I longingly watch the children playing
And feel my body warm when I catch you smiling

When I close my eyes, I can see it

I see the sky, clear and blue
The streaks of color fly by, as the wind takes the
leaves with it

I see the ground swaying beneath our feet
I hear the squeaking of the hammock
And the crickets in the distance
I hear your heart beating
As I push my ear closer to you chest
I smell your fabric softener, I smell your shampoo
As I close the space between my face and yours
I feel the sway of the world, as we are suspended
above it
I feel your beard, as you kiss my forehead
I feel flutters as you continue to hold me
I watch the leaves fall, as I fall more in love with you

When I close my eyes, I can see it

Same house, different snowstorm
Same couch, different fire
Same man, different movie
I still smell the scent of your soap, and the smell of
fire
I can feel your chest rise and fall
And your hands still drawing those endless circles
Same hands, same circles, different place
I watch the fire making shapes of its own
The light illuminating the mantle below three
stockings
I watch as your eyes leave the television to track my
body
As your thumb now draws circles on my growing
belly

When I open my eyes, I can see you
I can see us
And I can see our future

Top down, sunglassess on, and windy hair
Nightclub vibe, flashing lights, we're scantily bare

Drive upon an open road and sing Taylor karaoke
with me
Fill my nights with pillow talk and your vast
arrangement of tea

Sip on wine and last minute decide to shop for some
ice cream
At like a fool and break all the rules, we're as cool as
Cosmo magazine

You're my favorite distraction, know way more about
fashion, and always save me from self-destruction
I owe my best memories to you, and your rose-
colored hue, you are the deluxe edition

So here's to you, my best friend and my muse, my
beautiful platonic love
Til death do us part, I love you with all my heart, and
even as ghosts I will follow you

All I asked was for him to try
To be enough
For years, all I asked was for effort
Now all I ask, is for you

He gave me the effort
But still I ask for you
Because you gave effort, and I didn't have to ask

Madness is descending. Oh, how sweet it is.

Achingly ambiguous, but I'll bite anyway.

Kaleidoscopically captivating,

It enraptures and then breaks at the slightest misstep.

Nauseatingly beautiful, irresistible, inescapable; I try
and I try.

Games of pursuit transform into chasing the sound of
little feet

Leaving a legacy of love, however, requires
demonstration.

Operating rooms claw at the trauma and shame until
I am bare and raw.

Veins finally void of the poison that hitherto stunted
me.

Embracing now, my new soul. The one created, by
making love.

53

MOMENTS

A moment can change a lifetime
In one moment, I chose you
In one moment, I chose a million lifetimes with you
In one moment, I was running into your arms
Driving to your house
Turning to your lips
And taking your last name

I play this exact moment out in my head
When I would jump into your arms
And tell you I was yours
We would be lovers for the rest of our lifetime
Consoling each other in one moment
And celebrating in the next
This one moment would be the end of our goodbyes
A single moment will change our lives

This one moment never came
How different would our lives be if it had?

What a peculiar thing
To be walking down that generational path
The only one you've ever known
And yet somehow
That path crossed yours
Hidden and obscure as it was
It's there

It doesn't add up
The colors don't mix right
The logic isn't there
But here you are anyway
Like the dreams I used to have
Before life showed me
I deserved nothing
But the horrors I was dealt

You shouldn't be here
With that smile
Cutting through my drugged haze
With your laugh
Igniting a spark
In the soul I thought was long gone
Your eyes seeing something pure
When you look at me
Though my own reflection is dead

It's wrong
But I let your hand graze mine anyway
I let the unspoken gazes linger
I create a window in my boarded up house
Just big enough to peek through
And it hurts
The Hope
It's like razor sharp knives in my back
It's like stepping on Legos strapped to dynamite
Every cell in my being says to run
Like it has taught me time and time again

But there is something about you
It makes me feel alive again
To be alive is to be in pain
Yet being with you is like being on ecstasy
I crave your touch
I like who I am when I'm with you
Your dreams are my dreams
My demons are yours too
You take my bad days
And remind me of the good ones

And when my mind tells me
My bad days are who I truly am
When the past comes back
To pull me down the old rabbit-hole
You prove that I am different
And special
And worthy
And loved

Life, what a peculiar thing

CONCENTRATE

Tracing your jawline with my fingertips
Fingers laced through your hair
Drawing circles on your hand
While the circles of my eyes dilate
Foreheads pressed, heart full, mind empty
Extremities are trembling, faltering my self control
I can barely concentrate

Tracing your jawline with my eyes
Following the line to your mouth
Desires are exposed, as is my heart, my soul
Fragile and shallow breathing
Too afraid to move for fear of waking
I can't even concentrate

Tracing your jawline with my lips
Falling because I want to, trembling because I have to
Hands intertwined to match our hearts
My chest tightens and longs to shorten the distance
to yours
100 percent satisfied, but still 100 percent craving
You are my concentration

Tracing your lips with my own
Gentle, soft, lacking any hesitation, subtle
intoxication
Your tongue parts my lips, leaving enough room for
my gasp
Your hands, your lips, your grip, are all equally as
smooth against me
My lips close as my thighs part
My concentration is yours

Tracing your jaw with my fingers
While my lips trace your body
When I'm done
You won't be able to concentrate

Sail a boat
Take a train
Steal a car
Fly a plane
I really don't care
As long as your destination is me

Give me pink skies
The smell of pine
Carnival rides
And sweet red wine
I really don't care
As long as your lips end up on mine

I just want to see
Your lazy smile
Next to a campfire
Reflecting in your eyes
I really don't care
As long as there are no more goodbyes

So come back to me
With scars no one can see
But we all know are deep
And that's why you can't sleep
I really don't care
What you had to do over there
As long as you make it home to me

The constantness of my silence
Leads you to complacency
Knee-deep in quicksand
A mirage of success built
Upon forever-accumulating
Small shattering moments
You can't even see
That we're no longer growing
No longer building
No longer loving
No longer living
I'm doing acrobatics
With absolutely no practice
Just trying to relate to you
All I discover is your echo of hollowness
Reverberating deep in the caverns
We once carved together
Back when we actually wanted to know each other
When we were young and too naive
To know it wouldn't last

I told someone today
As I took a deep breath
The balloon in my throat
Inflated until I choked
I remember how
That silenced me
So many times before
I kept breathing anyway
Until it burst like a bubble
And like water,
My words flowed

I took back an apology today
When the guilt reared it's head
For not saying something sooner
An eagle flew down
Sunk it's sharp talons deep into
The guilt that braided itself
With my intestines
It was ripped from my body
And flown far away
To rot in eaglets bellies

I was believed today
Like opening a beautiful love letter
My heart was heard and seen
For the first time
The past shame of being pitied
Dissipated
The hope and fear
Of a truly loving touch
Of a warm smile
Of space and silence
We're relieving

Maybe now
I can help someone tomorrow

The moment I ran
I knew
I'd be alone forever
But living in a house
Filled with more skeletons
Than pearls
Has taught me that
Loneliness is a virtue
Self-preservation
A necessity

Woven charms
Welcome mats
Seasonal wreaths
Dressed up closed doors
What's beautiful on the outside
Must be true within
Like buying a clean and shiny
Used car
Without thinking
To check under the hood
After all
Everyone is smiling

I dreamed a dream
I planned a plan
Then ran and jumped
Without a second thought
I finally felt alive
Falling to my death
The unknown more comforting
Than the familiarity of eggshells
I knew
This would be the end for me
So, when I flew
I cried
And I laughed
Then I cried

Because I didn't recognize
The sound of my own happiness
So I laughed again
And relished the noise
Promised myself
I'd never forget again
Even though
I'd be alone forever

Well
Forever isn't that long
When deep baby blues
And perfect cupids bow
And tiny little toes
And your little button nose
Were copied and cloned
Onto the most beautiful soul
And now her laugh
Swallows you whole
And you think you might implode
At the thought of squeezing
One more drop of love
Into your bursting heart
There's no way
You can make a home
Filled with less skeletons
Than pearls
But you know
She deserves the world
And she deserves your best
You just have to trust
That all the rest
Will fall into place
Like it did
When you jumped
And you fell into
Yourself

Did your breath catch
When you saw me
Like mine did
When I first saw you?
Even now, I still find
I'm chasing breath when you're around

I wonder if the morning holds its breath
Until it sees you too

I curl into position
Knees into my chest
Better known as "fetal"
And I let myself cry
He's not around anyways

I curl into position
The test doesn't lie
The bed is still empty
But now I am not

I curl into position
It's harder now with my growing belly
Can I do this on my own?
He's not around anymore

I curl into position
The pain rocks across my body
I close my eyes
Open my legs
I hear her cry
For once I'm not crying alone

I curl into position
I wrap my body around hers
She smells like me
We are alone in the bed
And finally I am complete

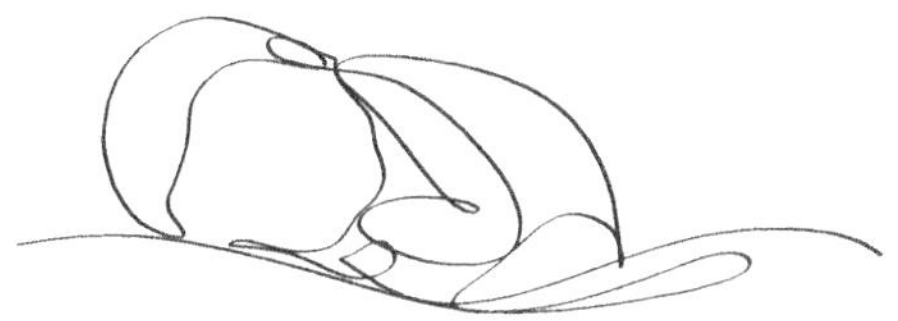

Have you ever been so happy to be so sick?
To be cradling the bowl,
Yet smiling through the heaves.
Excited to, one day, feel the flutters
That are causing your demise.

You wanted this.
You craved this.
You prayed and you cursed,
And you cried and you tried.
You smiled when people would ask,
And politely answered their questions
As you died inside, more each time.

You did everything right.
Your body became a temple fit for a God.
Your brain became so full of knowledge,
That you could teach a classroom full of teenagers.
Your heart became open and hopeful,
Waiting to be overflowed
With a love you could only dream of.

You bought the tests.
You tracked the color and texture
You worshipped the calendar
And you made sure to orgasm each time.
Then you'd leave your legs high in the air,
While you dreamed of your nose and his eyes.

You followed all the rules for months,
And recieved a cruel heartbreak each time.
The blood would flow, and so your tears...
Until this time.
Finally,
There were two pink lines.

She holds her belly tight
And never sleeps on her back at night

Dreaming of the day you'll both be born
Now a mom, her body exhausted and torn

She doesn't know your name, or even your face
But she can't wait to see it, or to embrace

The innocence that has captured her body and mind
for almost nine months
And somehow has changed her world suddenly, and
all at once

Soon her entire world would change, but for tonight
She holds her belly tight

Imagine this: Staring at a reflection and not
recognizing the person inside
Wondering when your eyes became encircled in rings
composed of black pigment
Attempting to tame the hair that is now wiry, that
you haven't washed all week
Staring at your engorged breasts that lay lifeless on
your encroaching belly

Your mind isn't as sharp as it used to be
The energy you had just months ago is gone
You're in bed by 8pm almost every night
God...you're as pathetic as you sound
With every passing day you look at a version of
yourself you don't connect to
Each night you stare at photos of your flat tummy
from just months ago

With every passing day, you lose another part of
yourself
The sacrifices have already begun
You offer up your beauty, your figure, your mind,
your energy, to someone you've never met
You happily give away tiny pieces of your heart,
body, and mind
Until one day you can hold a perfect reflection of
yourself in your arms

I get to see a little bean jumping all around on a
black and white screen
I get to hear the fast little flutter then feel the kicks
at week eighteen
I get to take on all the pain in the world before my
body finally concedes
I get to hear your small cries and hold you close as
we succumb to the relief

I get to watch you month by month as you reach each
milestone
I get to kiss your chubby cheeks and toes to make
sure you never feel alone
I get to teach you all the silly faces while you mimic
what you're shown
I get to sing you all the nursery rhymes that play
repeatedly on my phone

I get to feel the joy you radiate when you're giggling
so hard you can't breathe
I get to hold you when your storm is raging,
threatening to carry you out to sea
I get to rock you in my arms each night and watch
you while you dream
I get to share my favorite ice cream with you and
teach you to say "please"

I get to see your excited smile on your first day of
preschool
I get to wipe your little tears when you learn that
some kids can be cruel
I get to see you show your cleverness when you're
testing all the rules
I get to fall for all your jokes and laugh as you say
"April Fools!"

I get to see your whole world change as you grow
into your teens
I get to hand you two spoons and our favorite ice
cream when you start to feel unseen
I get to hug you when your heart gets broken and tell
you they're dumb and mean
I get to scream your name when you graduate and
watch you go off to chase your dreams

I get to meet each person you date and hope you find
the one
I get to celebrate all of your accomplishments as you
soar just short of the sun
I get to see you glowing on your wedding day as your
new life has just begun
I get to see who you've become through all the trials
and the fun

I get to be there when you grow your family up to
number three
I get to answer your daily phone calls, especially
when your day was crappy
I get to be there every day, from the very first until
you bury me
I'm lucky I get to love every version of you and every
version you will ever be

You are so pretty
How are you so brave?
Where'd you learn to be so smart?
You always know just what to say
When I am down
I know you'll always be around

I'll watch you pick out your clothes and do your
makeup everyday
I'll see you smile and wave to our nosy neighbors,
You always show them grace
And my little heart will race when I see you stand
your ground,
But I'll be proud

You're the best chef, most caring doctor
Safest chauffeur, best stray adopter
You're best actress when we play together
Have the most healing hugs when I'm overwhelmed
You're the smartest teacher and kindest person
You love everyone, especially me
And everyone loves you,
But not as much as I do

You are my mother
And you are everything to me

A sleek whiteboard, clean and new
A best-selling novel, not yet written
Identity stripped before it could be established
So, you're nothing

You didn't know the rules
Or that some don't abide by them
Caught in the crosshairs
You didn't know you were the bait

Your story was burned before you had the chance to
develop it
Your dreams were crushed before your subconcious
got to create them
You were never treated as the main character in your
life
And so you didn't know you are a star

Sorry they mistook sharpies for expos
And covered you in undeserved tattoos
Even if you had the means to remove them,
The painful scars will still remain
So you add more ink, and much more scarring
To shield the world, and yourself, from their shame

I want to love you
If you'll let me
I don't expect your love in return
And that's okay
I know you can't believe me
But you're safe here
I will protect you fiercely
And when you're ready to rewrite your novel
I will give you a pen and smile when you shine

Loss is inevitable

High school friends share everything with each other
Making promises they'll be best friends for life
Until high school is over and life moves on

Mothers push themselves to the brink of death
Just to give birth to a life who will one day leave
them

Lovers bear their souls to one another
And break things as they explore
Then decide that's not what they want anymore

Loved ones will pass on
Whether you knew it was coming or not
And the helplessness you feel
When a loss is so permanent is
Overwhelming

People come and people go, like clouds in the sky
And like clouds, some people bring rain, or hail, or
beautiful pink-orange sunrises
We know for a fact that one day everyone will leave
us
Yet we still can't seem to prepare ourselves for it

Grief strikes like a lightening bolt to the heart
The waves overcome us like a tsunami
We scream, but no one can hear us
Because what they hear is "I'm okay"
As they pass yet another casserole through the
threshold

They say time heals
But really it just makes you numb
Because one day something strikes a nerve you
thought had been barricaded off
And it's like that loss is happening all over again
And all we can do is close our eyes and face the sky,
and whisper

"I miss you"

I wake before the sun
With a head as clear as ice
The thought of having zero thoughts
I thought would be quite nice

But I taste the cold
And feel the dark
The moment I wake up
It's like my body misses you
Before I can catch up

My body is starving
I'm dying of hunger
People are well aware
And they're sending thoughts and prayers
The solution is simple, instead send food
However, they aren't in the mood to care
People keep saying I just need a distraction
They think I'm lying, looking for a reaction

My body is starving
I'm dying of hunger
Try as I might, I can't think of anything else
The emptiness inside me is painful and lonely
I can't even forget for a second
And suddenly I'm hyper-aware
There's cheese and bread and fruit everywhere
It's covered in mold and reeks of spoil
But I have the urge to consume it in heaves
The temptation is strong, but I have to be stronger
Someone will help, I believe

My body is starving
I'm dying of hunger
It's been weeks with no reprieve
The compulsion to eat this rotten meat has become
my new instinct
I start carefully and really slow, and I can see others'
disgust
"I have no other choice", I think to myself
And I slowly eat until I'm stuffed
For a brief moment, hunger pains went away and I
thought that maybe it was over
But not to long after, the affects of my binging came
doubling back in droves
"Help me!", I cried
I don't want to die
But still, everyone ignored my pleas

My body is buried
"She died by suicide"
My eulogy will read
They'll say "What a shame"
But still go on about their day
And won't think twice about the hand they played

All will be well
All will be alright
All will be fine

What if I don't want fine?
What if I've tasted perfection
And good isn't good enough

You have a piece of me
And what if I don't want to stumble around feeling
incomplete

What if what I want is more
More than fine
More than alright
More of you

A tune of promised love
Enticing, innocent
Sweet foreboding death
She calls in waves of sleepy lullabies
A slow slumbering trance
Willing, but not sure why

She catches your breath upon sight
As the dark world melts away
And bubbles escape into ecstasy
Cold and frozen, a melody of warmth
There is nothing to notice, but her
There is no pain in Nirvanna

Your body begs you to fight
For light, and air, and life
But you love it here in her illusion
In your deprivation of senses
In her enchanting canticle
And you submit as she consumes you

In this house there are three rooms,
I can move freely between them but I cannot leave
this place

The first room is completely empty, I call it
numbness. Numbness is desirable
I like and often choose numbness
If I could feel nothing at all then I feel no pain
It might be dangerous but its necessary to function

The second room has no light and happiness does not
exist here, I call it depression.
It's a nice room to be in, it's selfish
Depression is where I cry and scream until my
circulation quits and my hands turn blue,
Depression is where I wish my circulation would quit
for good
Depression tells me I am unloved and alone but at
least I'm not numb

The third room is white and fluffy
I call it denial,
In denial I play make-believe, pretend it was only a
fight
Pretend he didn't put his hands on me, I forget the
threats. In denial, he's not the bad guy- I made this
happen.
In denial I am the stupid bitch he called me and
that's okay

In this house I'm never happy

I do not want to be
Somewhere that I am not wanted
I've been around a lot of places
Trying to find where I fit in
Squeezing into spaces
That were never made for me
Changing every facet
Of my personality
Ignoring what I like or want
Because it doesn't match society
Trying so fucking hard
Just to realize that no one cares
What happens when
I am not wanted anywhere
What happens when
All that's left is
I do not want to be?

You think I don't know
You keep a chain in your pocket
With a small candid photo
In a family heirloom locket
You view it like a pocket watch
Ticking away the hour-long seconds
Since the veil separated us

You were the tortoise
I, the hare
Your consistent insistence
On slow and steady
Ended the chase
I forfeited the race long ago
Now you carry me on your strong back
So I can finally catch my breath

Pinkies and promises
Of rings on fingers
Lace and wine
Under Van Gogh skies
Bubbles and candles
Curled inside a clawfoot tub
Off-key belting
Piggie-backs on the beach
Flour on your nose
And batter on my cheek
A birthday cake in the oven
So bad we couldn't even eat

Then one day
All it took
Was a simple drive
One hand on my thigh
And a guy that was too high
To prove that
The effortlessness of Happily Ever After
Does not exist in this universe

You'll always be
My favorite "What if"

You know my name
You call here a lot
To tell me about your day
Well, the bad parts and what not
I open my ears
To hear about your story
I hang your trauma around my neck
Like it's an accessory

I extend my empathy
To it's fullest limit
But you'll take and take
If time will permit
Reject a piece of myself
In order to adopt your pain
Only for you to call again tomorrow

This is your addiction
It's as destructive as cocaine
You pile on your hurt
Until my soul starts to throb
Keeping you alive
Is somehow my job

I know your name
Your birthday and your address
I memorized it to repeat it to dispatch
Every time you need me to redress
You don't make good choices
And its me who winds up destroyed

The sky is black
The grass is brown
Like the dirt all over me
There's blood all around
What did I do?
I chastise myself
Of all the inconsequential choices
Which ones led me here with you?
Breathing so shallow
It's indiscernible
Heartbeat so slow
There is no pulse
The shock keeps me
From comprehending
What about you?
Twigs in my hair
I ignore the urge to pick them
A scream in my throat
I ignore the urge to release it
Salty sadness in my eyes
I ignore the urge to let it fall
How am I going to get out of this?
A body dragged through the woods
Puts an ache in muscles
You didn't know existed
But this ache is nothing
Compared to the pain left
From years of emotional scars
If I come out of this alive
He'll have me believe I deserved this
I brought it on myself
Despite all logic
I'll believe him
Then we'll pretend
That nothing is amiss

He'll bring me flowers
And kiss my cheek
Slathered in full coverage
To hide how bleak
My future is
Not to worry
I assure myself
If I let him bury me
I'll breathe in the sweet relief
Of earth and death
And happiness
Of all my inconsequential choices
What choice will I make tonight?

YOU'RE A LIFESAVER

A deflated lifesaver is sinking with me beneath
choppy waters
I've resolved myself to settle here
Where the fire raging in my lungs keeps me warm
And the darkness swallows me whole
I'm here alone
It won't be long now
Or so I thought

I see you in the distance
I hear your screams
You're hurting too
Through the blackness, I can clearly see
You've still got fight left in you
I remember when that used to be me

I use the remaining oxygen in my body to inflate the
tube
I put it around you
As the distance widens, you are my only focus
My eyes close
And you float to the surface

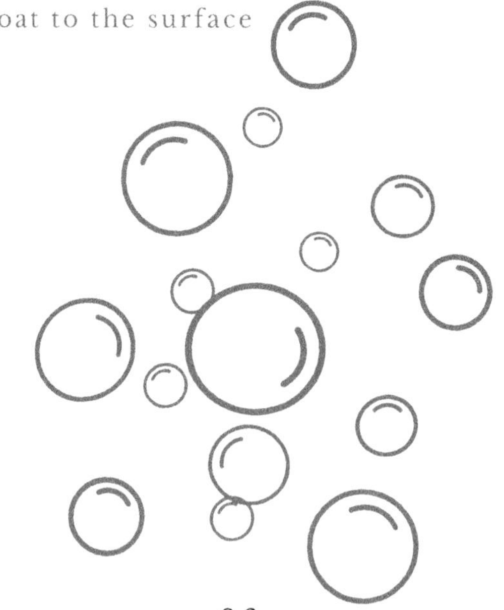

National Suicide Hotline: 800-273-8255

National Domestic Violence Hotline: 800-799-7233

National Eating Disorders Hotline: 800-931-2237

National Sexual Assault Hotline: 800-656-4673

SAMHSA National Helpline: 800-662-4357

The Trevor Project - LGBTQ Hotline: 866-488-4386

Find a counselor:
https://www.nbcc.org/search/counselorfind